CREATIVE WAYS TO LOVE & ENCOURAGE HIM

ALYSSA BETHKE

Published in Kihei, HI, by Bethke Writings. Bethke Writings titles may be purchased in bulk for educational, business, fund-raising, or sales promotional use. For information, please e-mail info@bethkewritings.com.

Unless otherwise noted, Scriptures are taken from the Holy Bible, New International Version®,NIV®. Copyright © 1973, 1978, 1984, 2011 by Biblica, Inc." Used by permission of Zondervan. All rights reserved worldwide. www.zondervan.com.

The Library of Congress Cataloging-in-Publication Data is on file with the Library of Congress ISBN-13: 978-0692720370

HOW TO GET THE MOST OUT OF THIS BOOK.

First off, you rock. By getting these paired books and wanting to go through them with your significant other, you obviously are already dominating at life! We have prayed over this project and really believe it can be a fun way to cultivate a healthy relationship and bring back the joy and intimacy that sometimes gets lost amidst the every day activities.

To get the most out of this book, we'd first say lean in. Lean into the ideas, the spontaneity and the parts that stretch you the most. Don't be afraid to just go for it, have fun and create memories. We are firm believers that with these two books, whatever you put into it you will get out of it. Isn't that true with all our relationships as a whole? Also know that this is just a template. Some things won't fit for your relationship or you can't do based on certain locations, resources and other variables.

We have tried to make every day as applicable for everyone as possible. So with that being said, feel free to morph it, change it, adapt it and do whatever you need to do to get the most out of it. Because at the end of the day, the goal isn't to follow this book rigidly and "cross each day off your checklist" but rather it's to bring a fresh vibrancy and life back to your relationship.

Also, a quick note to the dating folks out there. Obviously we are married so we are coming from that perspective. We also wanted to write this so dating couples could have a useful tool! As mentioned above, you might have to morph it in a different way too. When not living together, some of these are a little harder since when you're dating you probably don't see each other every single day. So feel free to stretch this out over a few months or pick a couple per week.

JEFF & ALYSSA BETHKE

DAY ONE:
PRAYER

Hands down the best thing you can do for your man is pray for him. I know a lot of times I'm tempted to do something else, something "better" or more noticeable. Which doing other things are great and totally part of pursuing him-hence this book! But prayer needs to be the foundation. I can't tell you how many times I've prayed for Jeff and then have been amazed at how God has moved in his heart. But even more so, I think prayer is what moves my heart to love and pursue him. I've found that when I'm consistently praying for Jeff, I'm way more patient, kind and gentle with him; I find myself cheering him on, being intentional and putting him above myself. A lot of times too, I don't know how to pursue Jeff. What could I do to show him I love him? That I'm thinking of him today? Lately, when I've asked the Lord to show me how to serve and love him, He leads me to do something for Jeff that ends up totally blessing Jeff that day. God knows our men the best, so why don't we ask Him to show us how to love them?

I will be the first to admit that I'm not consistent with praying for him, but I so long to grow in this area because when I do, it rocks! I think the lie that we can believe about prayer is that it's too easy, it won't do anything, we can do it better than God or we're just lazy. But the Lord loves it when we talk with Him. It doesn't need to be perfect, planned out or "spiritual." It just has to be real. You can talk to God about what you're hoping for your man, areas you'd love to see him grow in, questions you have or pray verses over him. I'll give you some verses today to get you started. Let's begin this journey with uplifting our men before our Father who is the One who knows and loves him the best.

Ephesians 6:10-20: Pray that he'd put on the armor of God today, being well suited for the spiritual battle that he faces each day.

Psalm 24:4: Pray that he'd be pure in heart, clinging to what is good and hating what is evil. Pray that he'd fight against any temptation to look or think on lustful thoughts.

Pray that he'd have wisdom as he goes about his day today, making decisions.

JOURNAL BELOW:

WRITE WHAT YOU LEARNED TODAY, HOW IT
WENT AND WHAT MEMORIES WERE MADE.

DAY TWO: SCRIP‐TURE

Scripture is full of prayers and songs of praises! Throughout the Old Testament we see men and women talking to God and giving Him praise for all that He's done. Then, in the New Testament, we read letters written by the apostles that have prayers written out that they're praying for believers in certain towns and cities. Many times, those same prayers have been my prayers for my family, friends and myself. I love praying through certain verses, because as I do so, it draws me closer to knowing who the Lord is as well as gives me wisdom in how to pray for those I love. Because truth be told, sometimes I just don't know what to pray for.

Going along with yesterdays call to action, today I'd like you to choose a verse to memorize and pray over your man for this next month. Maybe it's a verse you've been reading about lately, or something that the Lord lays on your heart. Write it out and frame it. Give it to your man, telling him you're praying this verse over him this month. Even if he doesn't know how to respond to this gesture, or doesn't say much, I know it'll really touch his heart knowing you're praying for him.

JOURNAL BELOW:

WRITE WHAT YOU LEARNED TODAY, HOW IT WENT AND WHAT MEMORIES WERE MADE.

DAY THREE: SERVICE

Galatians 5:13b, "...serve one another in love."

Jeff's all time favorite thing is getting his feet massaged. If there is one way I can serve him, it's that. If we're debating over something and we decide to bet on it, if I throw out that I'll massage his feet if I lose, he's all in! If I don't know what to get him for Christmas, I always have lotion and a foot massage to lean back on. It's just the best in his book. And if I'm totally honest with you, I have to talk myself in to doing it every time because GROSS. I mean, I adore my husband, but touching feet isn't on my list of favorite things to do. However, when I see how much Jeff loves it, it gives me joy. I love being able to serve him in this way; in a way that I know really blesses him. It helps him relax and shows him that I'm thinking of him.

Today, give your man a foot massage (or back if he likes that better). It doesn't have to be a 60-minute massage from the Four Seasons! Even just 5 minutes shows them that you are thankful for him and his hard work.

JOURNAL BELOW:

WRITE WHAT YOU LEARNED TODAY, HOW IT WENT AND WHAT MEMORIES WERE MADE.

DAY FOUR: SNACK TIME

The other day Jeff was taking a nap but I knew he'd be getting up soon and he'd need a little snack because dinner was still a ways off. I looked in our fridge and there were celery sticks already cut up. So I decided to just throw together some ants on a log (celery with peanut butter and raisins). OK, I didn't "just throw them together." They're actually a little more time consuming than I realized! Thanks, mom, for all those hours you spent making me them growing up! When Jeff woke up, he was a little cranky. I'm just being real with ya'll here. I mean, let's be honest, sometimes you wake up from a nap feeling like you just won the lottery. And other times you feel worse than when you fell asleep. This was the latter for my man that day. But then when he saw the ants on a log on the kitchen counter waiting for him, his whole face lit up and his entire demeanor changed. He ate those bad boys, and was a whole new man.

Today, make or put together your man's favorite snack. If your man loves pistachios, just buy a bag for him at the store, he will love it! Or it can be super simple like cut up apple slices or microwavable popcorn. Just think of something that he likes and have it ready for him when he gets home or when you see him today.

JOURNAL BELOW:

WRITE WHAT YOU LEARNED TODAY, HOW IT WENT AND WHAT MEMORIES WERE MADE.

_____

_____

_____

DAY FIVE: DINNER TIME

Whoever said, "Food is the way to a man's heart," hit it right on the head! No truer words have been said when it comes to my husband. He loves eating and he loves food, good food. (I mean, who am I kidding? SO DO I!) If you ever come to our house for dinner and we are eating something that Jeff loves, he'll give me a standing ovation and bang his hands on the table (sure makes a girl feel good). Kinsley, our 2 year old daughter, does the same thing now when she likes something. It's too cute!

I'm guessing that for the majority of us, your man likes food too. And even if he isn't a foodie, I know he appreciates a good meal that is provided for him. This week, plan to make him a dinner that he really enjoys. For some of you, this totally excites you! You love to cook. You're pulling out your Pioneer Woman recipe books, scrolling through Pinterest to find the perfect meal. Others of you are probably wanting to ignore this whole mention of making dinner and skip ahead because cooking is just not something you do or enjoy. So I'm just gonna say this-grace and freedom on you!! If you love to cook, then you go girl! You get at it! But if it's not your thing, that's OK. You don't have to be Martha Stewart in the kitchen. Either make something really simple or go grab take out from one of his favorite restaurants. There's nothing to prove to him or yourself. It's just showing him you care by providing a good meal. (And if that good meal is a happy meal from McDonald's because that's what he likes, then awesome!)

JOURNAL BELOW:

WRITE WHAT YOU LEARNED TODAY, HOW IT
WENT AND WHAT MEMORIES WERE MADE.

DAY SIX: PRAY FOR YOUR MAN

I'm longing to grow in praying for Jeff more consistently. When he's traveling, I find myself praying for him much more often, probably because we don't talk nearly as much. So I take my concerns and his heart to the Lord instead of just relying on myself to love him. But when we're home together, I often forget to pray for him because I'm talking to him all the time and I think I just take him, or rather the fact that I'm with him all the time, for granted. It's easy for me to pray for everything else, like my kids, my worries or friends, over him. Why is that? But on top of just longing to pray for him more, I also want to grow in praying over him; when he's right there besides me, to put my hand on him and lift him up to the Father. Sometimes when Jeff's struggling with something, he'll come to me and ask me to pray for him. And every time, it's like I'm caught off guard. Like I forget that that's something God calls us to do. And every time I do it, it's so beautiful. Jeff is totally vulnerable with me, humble to ask for help, and I get to join with him, going to the Father with his concerns. What an honor!

On top of all that, whenever I'm having a hard day or just flat out so emotional, Jeff will always ask if he can pray for me. And it's one of the absolute sweetest things. I think it's the way I feel most loved from him. Because truth be told, sometimes I'm just way too weak to even ask Jesus for help (or maybe too prideful). And then Jeff steps in for me and asks on my behalf.

You get to have the same honor of praying for your man, while he's right there with you. It may feel awkward at first or you may be embarrassed or shy. But don't be! It is a huge privilege and one that will not only bless your man but also bring you two together as you go before the Father together.

Today, ask him if you can pray over him. It could be before he goes to work, before bed tonight or just in the middle of the day. Thank the Lord for this man of yours and pray for his heart and mind; for his work, protection and purity.

JOURNAL BELOW:

WRITE WHAT YOU LEARNED TODAY, HOW IT
WENT AND WHAT MEMORIES WERE MADE.

DAY SEVEN: ENTER HIS WORLD

Part of loving someone is doing what they love to do; *entering their world.* For instance, one way I show Kinsley that I love her is by intentionally playing with her. To do that, I need to enter her world and do what she loves to do. So, you may find me on all fours, crawling around our coffee table chasing her. Or, I may put on her princess crown and sit criss cross on the floor with all her stuffed animals surrounding us as I read a book to her. I don't do this all the time and I really do have to consciously think how I can be intentional with her somedays. But when I do it, not only does she love it, but I love it because I get to be a kid again and just love being with my little girl.

Guys are the same! One way that they bond with someone is by doing a shared activity. Jeff can go hiking, paddle boarding or shoot some hoops with another guy and automatically they're connected in some way. In relationships, I think it can be easy (especially in marriage) to forget this and to get into the habit of talking and then doing your own things. Right now Jeff and I are in the newborn stage with a toddler, we're exhausted a lot. We give all we have when our kids are awake, but by the time they go to sleep, we're so tired, we just go to bed ourselves. Or we sit on the couch doing our own things like reading or scrolling through Instagram and Facebook. And some nights, that's totally OK! But if we go a few nights in a row like that, we start to feel disconnected. So, we're trying to be more intentional with each other and one way for us to do that is for me to enter his world. What does Jeff like to do? And how can I hop in and do it with him?

Think of one thing that your man loves to do. It may be a sport, a certain genre of movie, a book that he's currently reading, working out, cooking, gardening, music, cars, etc. Today (or sometime this week) do that hobby *with* him. Go see that movie he's been dying to see with him in the theatre, go watch his softball game and cheer him on, pick up a copy of the book he's reading and read it together, listen to him play guitar, ask him to show you something about cars. Enter HIS world this week.

JOURNAL BELOW:

WRITE WHAT YOU LEARNED TODAY, HOW IT
WENT AND WHAT MEMORIES WERE MADE.

DAY EIGHT: BREAKFAST IS THE MOST IMPORTANT MEAL OF THE DAY

About 6 months into dating Jeff, he got a new job and had to travel a lot. I MEAN A LOT. Like every week. Some trips he would land in Seattle at 2pm and have to fly back out at 5pm that same night. To say it was hard for me is an understatement! I mean, I loved that he was loving what he was doing and was so filled up but man, I missed my guy.

For one of his trips, I got to drive him to the airport early that morning because I didn't have work that day. I hadn't seen him much, so we decided we'd stop at the nearest Starbucks by the airport for a quick coffee date before he flew out. Obviously Starbucks has coffee (mmmm coffee) and pastries but I wanted to make it a special little coffee break for us, so I whipped up some cream cheese peach muffins for Jeff. 1. Because he loves cream cheese 2. Because he loves anything peach. 3. Because I straight up love muffins. I put them in a basket with napkins and a note and brought them into Starbucks with us.

Looking back now that I'm married and know my husband, that was just a little appetizer for him, maybe even an appetizer to the appetizer! A muffin is just a snack to Jeff; he needs the full meal deal. Eggs, potatoes, toast. Regardless, he loved those muffins, but I think even more so, he loved that I *thought of him* and made something that had his favorites in it. And really, it didn't take that much of an effort on my part.

Today, think of a fun breakfast treat that your man would enjoy (muffins, cinnamon rolls, donuts, bagels, etc.). Meet up with him tomorrow morning and share your treat together. If that's not possible because he leaves so early, then leave it where he'll find it in the morning (or take it to his work) with a cute little note just saying you were thinking of him and you hope he has a great day.

JOURNAL BELOW:

WRITE WHAT YOU LEARNED TODAY, HOW IT
WENT AND WHAT MEMORIES WERE MADE.

_____

_____

_____

_____

_____

_____

_____

_____

_____

_____

_____

_____

DAY NINE: EYE CONTACT

Words are powerful. They can either build up or tear down. Words can either destroy a relationship or make it flourish. Jeff is so good about telling me every day that he loves me and is thankful for me. He constantly is telling me that I'm beautiful and a wonderful wife and mom. Can I be honest with you? Most of the time, especially lately, I sure don't *feel* beautiful. I probably already botched up being a wonderful wife and mom that day by a comment I made or by being impatient or selfish. But when Jeff looks me in the eyes and speaks those words over me, I start to believe them instead of getting bogged down by the lies I can so easily believe about myself. And that gives me life. It gives me hope. It helps me to see myself the way God sees me and it helps me to be a better wife and mom. Insecurities fly out the door. Feelings of being overwhelmed or anxious are exchanged for courage to do the task God's given me.

It can be easy to not speak life into our men because we're too busy but man, is it important! So today, look your man in the eyes and tell him how thankful you are for him and at least one thing that you love about him. Think of something specific like, "I love how you provide for our family" or "I love how you listen to people and make them feel heard."

JOURNAL BELOW:

WRITE WHAT YOU LEARNED TODAY, HOW IT WENT AND WHAT MEMORIES WERE MADE.

_____

_____

_____

DAY TEN: 10 THINGS

A few weeks ago I was praying for Jeff and had asked the Lord to show me how I could encourage him that day. It had been a week after I had given birth to our son Kannon, so I felt pretty tapped out and not able to do much for Jeff. I was getting ready in our bathroom and saw our dry eraser marker in a basket. You know, you never know when you need to write a little note on your bathroom mirror! So I grabbed that bad boy and wrote out 10 things I loved about Jeff on his side of the mirror. It took me probably 5 minutes. It wasn't pretty or designed or super thought out. It was just a little overflow of my heart letting him know that I love him, see him and am thankful for all he does. Later that day, I was sitting on our couch, when he came out and told me how much that list meant to him. It totally made his day! It was just a small gesture that made all the difference that day.

Today, write out 10 things that you love and appreciate about your man. Write it on his bathroom mirror, in a note or text.

JOURNAL BELOW:

WRITE WHAT YOU LEARNED TODAY, HOW IT WENT AND WHAT MEMORIES WERE MADE.

DAY ELEVEN: HOW HE'S GROWN

Life can be discouraging at times and we can get bogged down by thinking of all the things we aren't doing right, what we need to do differently, what we need to change or how we failed in a particular task or moment. I think too, often it's harder to see what God is doing in us or the ways we've grown. But God is always at work in our lives and we are always growing if we're seeking Him. There is always fruit, even if it's just a seed.

When you're doing life with someone, it's so important to point out areas you see them growing in because often they don't see it themselves. There is nothing like hearing someone, especially someone close to you, tell you you're doing an awesome job in this area or how you've become more patient, gentle or kind in this way. It's so encouraging and gives you hope that you are growing, even though you're not perfect and still have room to change.

Today, tell your man at least one area that you've seen him grow in lately and how proud you are of him. If you're not sure what that is, spend some time praying and thinking of the past couple of weeks. When you spend time praying for your man, you're more attuned to what God is doing in his life. *Note: When you tell him how he's grown today, don't tell him how bad he was before at something! Just mention how you've seen him be a certain way lately and how proud you are of him. For instance, "Babe, I've seen you be really patient with your clients this week and I'm so proud of you." Or "Thank you for taking out the trash this week without me even having to ask you. I so appreciate that. Thank you for being on it, and serving me in that way."

JOURNAL BELOW:

WRITE WHAT YOU LEARNED TODAY, HOW IT
WENT AND WHAT MEMORIES WERE MADE.

_____

_____

_____

_____

_____

_____

_____

_____

_____

_____

_____

_____

_____

_____

DAY TWELVE: RESPONSIBILITIES

I remember when Jeff and I first got married, we argued over making the bed for like the first two years! I love a made bed. It's my jam. When I'm getting things done, it's the first thing I do. I feel frazzled if it's unmade and I hate looking into our room if the bed is all messy. I'm totally OK leaving it unmade if we're running late somewhere, but otherwise, I like it nice and neat. Jeff on the other hand, thought it was a waste of time because we're just going to sleep in it that night and get it messy again. Can anyone else relate to this debate? We went back and forth forever. Then finally one day, Jeff got me. I wouldn't say he felt the same way about needing it to be made to get other things done or to feel organized but he realized that regardless of his opinion, the fact was that making the bed was important to me and it really served me to have it made. One day I walked in,and it was made. And I'll add that he did a better job at making it than I did!

For the most part, I still end up making the bed most of the time. But on those days that I walk into our room after breakfast and he's made the bed, I always stop and look and feel so loved in that moment. It's a small gesture, but I know that Jeff was thinking of me and did it for me. He knew that it would help and serve me to do it. And although it's his bed too, I know he did it for me because he doesn't really care about a made bed.

Today, think of a responsibility that he has and do it for him. It doesn't have to be something that you guys think differently about! Think of a task that he always does that you could do for him. It could be taking out the trash, washing his car, making his lunch for the next day, bringing snacks to his meeting so he doesn't have to, etc.

JOURNAL BELOW:

WRITE WHAT YOU LEARNED TODAY, HOW IT
WENT AND WHAT MEMORIES WERE MADE.

_____

_____

_____

_____

_____

_____

_____

_____

_____

_____

_____

_____

DAY THIRTEEN

CAR SUR-PRISES

Last week we celebrated Mother's Day. I had really been wanting eyelash extensions FOREVER, so I finally got them. Because who has time to put on make up with a toddler and newborn!? I told Jeff that was my Mother's Day gift. All that to say, I wasn't expecting anything on Mother's Day, I just wanted to be with my family and celebrate my mom. After we had a special breakfast and played in the yard, both the kids fell asleep (oh how I cherish you sweet nap time), so I told Jeff I was going to take a bath and lay down for a bit. While I was rocking Kins asleep in her room, Jeff went ahead and got my bath ready. He filled it with bath salts and bubble bath, lit a candle, put on music, grabbed my book and wrote a little note that said "I LOVE YOU." When I came out of Kinsley's room, I smelled the bath salts and went into the bathroom amazed. Talk about an amazing husband! How thoughtful was he!? You know the funny thing though? Amidst all that wonderfulness, my favorite part was the little note that said "I LOVE YOU." I know I'm a words person. I feel the most loved by written word. And I'll take it in any form-texts, emails, cards. But there was something just so sweet about seeing Jeff's handwriting on that bright blue card in bold font. I still have it hanging up in my bathroom mirror.

Little surprises that say "Hey, I'm thinking of you," are always sweet and special. It's such a good feeling to know that someone has you on his or her mind. And it can be the littlest thing! Today, put a little something in his car as a sweet surprise. It could be a little note that says "I LOVE YOU," your picture on his dashboard or his favorite candy bar. Anything that says you're thinking of him.

JOURNAL BELOW:

WRITE WHAT YOU LEARNED TODAY, HOW IT
WENT AND WHAT MEMORIES WERE MADE.

_____

_____

_____

_____

_____

_____

_____

_____

_____

_____

_____

_____

_____

_____

DAY FOUR-TEEN: MAKE IT KNOWN

If you're on Facebook or Instagram, I'm sure you've seen ladies post about their men and use #MCM (Man Crush Monday). Although I always forget to post about Jeff on Mondays just like I always forget to do a #TBT (Throw Back Thursday) until Friday-I love this concept! I think it's so great to tell others how thankful we are for our men, especially in a culture where women put down their men in front of others. Let's be women who speak kindly about our men, who honor them, respect them and cheer them on.

Today, post a Facebook or Instagram post about how thankful you are for your man. Use #31creativeways so we can all see it and cheer each other on as women who honor their men!

JOURNAL BELOW:

WRITE WHAT YOU LEARNED TODAY, HOW IT WENT AND WHAT MEMORIES WERE MADE.

_____

_____

_____

_____

_____

DAY FIFTEEN: OUR STORY

One of my favorite questions to ask a couple is how they met or when did they know that was the person they wanted to spend the rest of their lives with. The best is hearing the couple go back and forth, playing off of each other and hearing them recount their story. As they talk, you can still see the sparkle in their eye and by the end of the story, its like they are closer in some way. They are enjoying one another more than when they sat down because they're reminded of how sweet their story is and how much they love each other.

Bring a little sparkle back today by writing a note to your guy telling him your meeting story and when you started to fall for him. It can be a long letter or just a simple note to remind him of your beginnings.

JOURNAL BELOW:

WRITE WHAT YOU LEARNED TODAY, HOW IT
WENT AND WHAT MEMORIES WERE MADE.

DAY
SIXTEEN:
DREAMS

Jeff and I do this journal together where we ask each other the same 6 specific questions every week (well, we're trying to do it every week). It's a game changer. Truly. Talking about these questions each week helps us to get on the same page and breeds a lot more grace and support in our marriage. It gives us a vision for the week and a short-term vision for our relationship.

One of the questions we ask each other is, "What dreams or thoughts have been on your mind this week?" Now, my husband and I are both dreamers, so this question isn't too difficult for us. However, Jeff is an extreme visionary, so every week he has a *new* dream to share! Which at times can be hard for this anxious little heart of mine. Always something new. Always something changing. Always something in the works. The more I'm married to Jeff though, I'm realizing how important it is to really listen to him dreams and to encourage him in them. Even if it sounds crazy or totally 100% out of my comfort zone. I can share my questions, of course, but I need to cheer him on in it and dream with him first. When I do that, it's like he's a new man, fearless and able to conquer anything. But when I let my anxious heart get in the way and give him looks like, "Oh boy, another dream..." it completely crushes him.

I realize that Jeff is an extreme case of a dreamer and most likely your man doesn't always have a new thing on the horizon. However, all of us have dreams and all have us have thoughts throughout the week of something we're hoping to do, to accomplish, to change. For instance, in this season of my life right now, I don't have a whole lot of dreams that I'm thinking of. However, I want to have a certain couple over for dinner next week, I want to take Kinsley to the strawberry farm next weekend and I really want to join a barre class to tone up a bit. Thoughts. Dreams.

Today, ask your man a thought or dream that he's been chewing on this week. Something he can't stop thinking of or something that keeps coming back to his mind. Listen as he shares and dream with him. Encourage him in a certain endeavor or pray over it for him.

JOURNAL BELOW:

WRITE WHAT YOU LEARNED TODAY, HOW IT
WENT AND WHAT MEMORIES WERE MADE.

_____

_____

_____

_____

_____

_____

_____

_____

_____

_____

_____

_____

_____

DAY SEVENTEEN: CANDY CRUSH

When Jeff and I first started dating, it was long distance. He was in Oregon going to college and I was across the Pacific Ocean in Hawaii doing an internship at a church. Although long distance definitely has it pits-like you're not together! But one good thing is it forces you to be creative. Like really creative. I mean, when you can't hang out, go on dates or see each other at church, you're forced to find ways to show each other that you care other than the phone.

One Valentine's Day I decided to make Jeff a candy gram. I went to the store and bought as many different candy bars that I could find. Then I put a bunch of construction paper together like a book and wrote him a love letter using the candy bars as fill in words. Next thing I know, I'm getting a telephone call with Jeff on the other end, munching on a candy bar, proclaiming how awesome my candy gram was! HE LOVED IT.

Now, even if your man is super healthy or doesn't really do candy, I guarantee he'll love the candy gram because it's thoughtful and creative. So, go to the grocery store or gas station and pick up some candy bars to make your own candy gram for your man. Some good ones to get are *Symphony, 1,000 grand, Milky Way, Hot Tamales, & Big Hunk.* Make your message as short or as long as you like. You don't have to be a poet to do it! Just be creative and have fun.

JOURNAL BELOW:

WRITE WHAT YOU LEARNED TODAY, HOW IT
WENT AND WHAT MEMORIES WERE MADE.

_____

_____

_____

_____

_____

_____

_____

_____

_____

_____

_____

_____

_____

_____

DAY EIGHT-TEEN: LET'S GO ON A DATE

To this day, Jeff will still tell you that one of his all time favorite dates that I took him on was when he came out to Maui to visit me. My youth pastor had let me borrow his truck for the night, so I couldn't wait to take Jeff out somewhere. However, being an intern, I had no money. Like zilch. So I packed a special picnic dinner for us. You know, PB & J's, apples and cookies. I filled up two Nalgene bottles with water and added some crystal light peach packets in them because I knew how much Jeff loved peach flavoring. We drove down the street awhile and then parked where we could back up to the beach. We climbed in the back of the truck, put a blanket down and ate our picnic dinner as we watched the sun sink into the ocean. We talked, laughed and had the best time!

Plan a special date with your guy this week. It doesn't have to be elaborate or expensive, just something that is intentional and brings you two together. Think of something that *he* would love to do. If you need to get a babysitter, do it, or you can always do something when the kids go to bed. It doesn't even have to be that long. If you only can fit in an hour, that's perfect. You'll be surprised at how much you can pack into an hour when you're both being intentional with each other. Some ideas are: have a bonfire, play a board game, chat over a fruit and cheese platter.

JOURNAL BELOW:

WRITE WHAT YOU LEARNED TODAY, HOW IT WENT AND WHAT MEMORIES WERE MADE.

_____

_____

_____

DAY NINE-TEEN: SPECIAL PLACE

We all have our favorite places to go and hang out. They become "our places." Maybe you have a favorite coffee shop you like to hang out at, a store that you always go to or a park that you love to go and read at. For me, there's this walk down the road a bit that is right on the ocean. It's gorgeous, truly breathe taking. It's about 1.5 miles long and lines up with all the resorts on the water. It curves and has hills and is lined with tropical greenery. As you walk you can see all the boats and ships that go sailing by. Some days you can spot whales out in the ocean deep or turtles swimming by the shore. It's my all time favorite place in the whole world. I've spent countless hours walking that path praying, dreaming, processing and having heart to hearts with friends.

Jeff has never been someone to go for walks. He likes working out but not if it feels like working out! Give him basketball, paddle boarding or swimming, anything that's fun and action packed. But recently he's been up for walking with me. I used to have to beg him to come with me but now if I mention I'm going on a walk, half the time he jumps at the chance to go with me! And I can't tell you how much it means to me. I love having that intentional time with him and I love the fact that he's wanting to join me on something I love doing. So, when he goes with me on my favorite walk, it's like he's shouting from the rooftops, "I LOVE YOU ALYSSA!"

Think of one of your man's favorite spots to hang out and go with him to that spot this week. If it's Crossfit or his gym, go watch him or buy a one-day pass to work out together. If it's a music store, go look at instruments together. If it's a food truck, go get lunch together. Whatever is his spot, go there together this week.

JOURNAL BELOW:

WRITE WHAT YOU LEARNED TODAY, HOW IT
WENT AND WHAT MEMORIES WERE MADE.

DAY TWENTY: OH, HEY HAND-SOME

Laughing is one of my favorite things to do. Tell me a good joke and it'll make my whole day. When I was in junior high, my friend and I use to send each other pick-up lines from this one website. We got the biggest kick out of the ones people came up with and bonus! The website had a new pick up line every day. I always wanted a guy to use one of the pick up lines on me. I mean, how could a girl say no to, "Looks like you dropped something- my jaw!"

Today, find a good pick-up line and use it on your guy. Text it, email it, write it in a note. Maybe even have a different one for him every hour! Whatever you do, show him you like him while giving him a good laugh.

JOURNAL BELOW:
WRITE WHAT YOU LEARNED TODAY, HOW IT WENT AND WHAT MEMORIES WERE MADE.

_____

_____

_____

_____

_____

_____

DAY TWENTY-ONE: MOVIE NIGHT

Jeff and I love our movie nights. We don't get to the movie theatre much these days but one of our favorite things to do is pick a good movie on Netflix or Amazon and cuddle up on the couch together. Jeff makes this crazy good popcorn that we put in our special white popcorn bowls and Aslan, our dog, sits by my feet drooling the whole time I chomp away.

As I am writing this, I'm realizing that for the most part, we always watch a movie that I want to watch. Now, don't get me wrong. Jeff will agree to the movie and want to watch it too but it's never one on the top of his list. He always goes ahead with one that I really want to see because he's so sweet and because I'm a lot more picky movie watcher. I mean, I just really love my Rom Coms (romantic comedies)! This week, watch a movie with your man but let him choose the movie. Pop some popcorn, get some candy and cuddle up together.

JOURNAL BELOW:

WRITE WHAT YOU LEARNED TODAY, HOW IT WENT AND WHAT MEMORIES WERE MADE.

_____

_____

_____

_____

_____

DAY TWENTY-TWO: ART OF THANK YOU

One thing that makes for a successful relationship is found in two words- "THANK YOU." Showing that you notice what he's doing and are grateful is monumental in a relationship. It shows that you see him and you appreciate him. Sometimes it can be easy to get caught up in all the things that he's not doing or ways you wish he would change. But that can be toxic.

When Jeff says thank you to me for doing the things that I normally do everyday, it makes me want to keep serving him and gives me joy in the midst of it. Sometimes he'll stop me from what I'm doing, look me in the eye and thank me for something specific. It makes me break out in the biggest smile; it's the best.

This week, focus on saying thank you for the big and little things that your man does. For taking out the trash, clearing your plate, opening your door, making you coffee, etc. Today specifically, think of one thing he's done for you, look him in the eye and say thank you.

JOURNAL BELOW:

WRITE WHAT YOU LEARNED TODAY, HOW IT WENT AND WHAT MEMORIES WERE MADE.

_____

_____

_____

_____

DAY TWENTY-THREE: DRAW A PICTURE

Last weekend we celebrated Kinsley's 2nd birthday. Since Kinsley's favorite thing in the whole world is swimming, we bought her a blow up pool complete with a slide and ball activities. We had a little pool party with a few of her closest friends. She had a blast! Literally it was the best day of her life. She giggled and smiled the whole morning. Her friends all brought her a little gift and all of them included a homemade card. Her friend Ace drew her a stick picture of the two of them together and handed it to her as soon as he saw her. She looked at it, pointed to each stick figure and got the biggest smile on her face.

Cards can sometimes be the best gift of all. I love how little kids draw pictures for people. I have a handful hanging up on my refrigerator right now, displayed as the pieces of artwork that they are.

This may sound silly, but draw a picture for your man today. If you're an incredible artist, then draw something amazing! But if you're like me and stick figures is about as good as it gets, that's OK too! Really, this days action is all about bringing the childlike wonder back into a relationship. It's just something fun and thoughtful. Draw it on a sticky note or construction paper. Draw a picture of your man and point out characteristics that he has that you love. Or draw a picture of the two of you together. Maybe draw a picture of when you met, your favorite date or one of your favorite memories. Or draw a picture of something you'd like to do together one day. Whatever it is, I'm sure he'll cherish it as Kinsley cherished her homemade birthday cards.

JOURNAL BELOW:

WRITE WHAT YOU LEARNED TODAY, HOW IT
WENT AND WHAT MEMORIES WERE MADE.

_____

_____

_____

_____

_____

_____

_____

_____

_____

_____

_____

_____

DAY TWENTY-FOUR: CHEER-LEADER

I hosted a mom's gathering this last spring with a handful of women who I really wanted to get know more. Each week they'd come over for a time of fellowship and learning. An older mom would come and share each week about what they have learned as a mom or wife or what God's taught them over the years. Not only did our group become tight-knit, we also got to be encouraged by these older women and shaped by their wisdom. One of the ladies who came to teach shared about loving and enjoying her husband. She told us that we as wives are called to be our husbands' biggest cheerleaders. We are to stand by their side, support them, listen well, pray diligently and encourage them. I had known to support and encourage Jeff but I had never heard it quite phrased that way before-be their biggest cheerleader. I love it that it gives me an awesome picture in my head of one of the main roles as a wife. Even if you're just dating, being a cheerleader for your man is important! Our guys need to know we believe in them and are for them.

Take a picture of yourself today, holding up a sign that says "GO ___(fill in your man's name)____!" Send it to him sometime today, letting him know that you are cheering him on!

JOURNAL BELOW:

WRITE WHAT YOU LEARNED TODAY, HOW IT WENT AND WHAT MEMORIES WERE MADE.

_____

_____

_____

DAY TWENTY-FIVE: BUCKET LIST

We have these friends who pretty much rock at life. They're some of my favorite people ever and a couple that I really look up to. Last year their church focused on loving and pursuing your spouse and encouraged their congregation to go on date with each other every week. They called it 52 in 15 (2015). As in, 52 dates in 52 weeks. At the end of the year, the couples that actually did 52 dates were entered into a contest to win a vacation cruise for a week. It's an awesome concept if you ask me! The whole purpose behind it is to encourage married couples to invest in their marriage. Well, this year, our friends are doing it again, but for their dates they made a bucket list; a list of 52 dates that they want to do with one another. It's been so fun to follow them on Instagram and see the fun dates they do. Some have been making a fruit pizza together, going on a picnic, and making a playlist that reflects their spouse.

Sit down with your guy today or sometime this week and make a bucket list of dates that you want to do together. You don't need to do 52! But get at least 10 down that the two of you can do together. Make the bucket list making a little date in itself! Get some yummy snacks, a good drink and have fun scheming together.

JOURNAL BELOW:

WRITE WHAT YOU LEARNED TODAY, HOW IT WENT AND WHAT MEMORIES WERE MADE.

_____

_____

_____

DAY TWENTY-SIX: COMPLI-MENTS

"Pleasant words are a honeycomb, sweet to the soul
and healing to the bones." Proverbs 16:24

Have you ever had someone give you a card or send you a random text that tells you how special you are and even has a little list of character traits you possess that they love and admire? It's the absolute best. And if you're like me, it usually comes at just the right moment that you need it.

My parents and friends would give me little notes growing up with these sweet sayings but the one I remember most was an unexpected card from one of my close friends and mentors when I was interning at the church. It had been a long, hard day and to be honest, I was in a season of a lot of growth. Which is a nice way of saying I was a hot mess! The Lord was stretching me and growing me in ways I'd never knew were possible. I walked into our office and there on my computer was an envelope with my name beautifully written on the top of it. I opened it up and there was a list of things she saw in me that were beautiful. Tears stung in my eyes because amidst all my mess, there was a deep beauty that God was creating and continuing to perfect in me.

Words can make all the difference in someone's day. Send a little text to your man today with at least 5 genuine things that you love about him.

JOURNAL BELOW:

WRITE WHAT YOU LEARNED TODAY, HOW IT
WENT AND WHAT MEMORIES WERE MADE.

_____

_____

_____

_____

_____

_____

_____

_____

_____

_____

_____

_____

DAY TWENTY-SEVEN: JUST ASK

This past year, Jeff has started to ask me before the day starts or after a heart to heart, what he can do to help me that day? How can he serve me today? And each time that he asks me, my heart softens and calms. Sometimes, I actually do have some things for him to do that would really be helpful to me. But for the most part, it brings me peace and encouragement that he just asks. It shows me that he's thinking of me and reminds me that we're a team. I'm not alone. I don't have to do everything on my own but he's there to help me in any way. Which, for me, is so encouraging because I tend to get overwhelmed easily.

Ask your guy if there's anything you can do to help him today. Is there any way you can serve him? Be prepared if he does have something for you to do and do it cheerfully! But know that just the asking will encourage him too.

JOURNAL BELOW:

WRITE WHAT YOU LEARNED TODAY, HOW IT WENT AND WHAT MEMORIES WERE MADE.

_____

_____

_____

_____

_____

DAY TWENTY-EIGHT: ABC

"ABC

It's easy as 1,2,3

As simple as do, re, mi

ABC 1,2,3

Baby, you and me girl."

Today's task will take a little more time and thought but I promise you it will be something that will really bless and honor him.

Pinterest is full of cute little ways to show your man you love him. One year for Valentine's Day I rummaged through a whole list of DIY ideas of things I could make for Jeff. I saw this deck of cards that they punched a hole through on top and put together. On each card, they had written a characteristic trait that they loved about their man. It was so cute! And so I went ahead and whipped (well, not quite!) one up for Jeff. I remember seeing the look on his face when he opened it and read each one. He was so touched that I had spent so much time coming up with 52 things that I love about him. It's still in his side table by his bed as a little reminder that I love him so.

For today's task, I won't ask you to come up with 52 things you love about your man (feel free too though)! However, 26 things seems pretty doable. Get 26 little cards together, 26 sticky notes or just a sheet of paper and write out the ABC's. Come up with a character trait or something that your man does that you love for each letter of the alphabet. It doesn't have to be poetic at all or even artsy. Just dot down 26 things you love about him.

JOURNAL BELOW:

WRITE WHAT YOU LEARNED TODAY, HOW IT
WENT AND WHAT MEMORIES WERE MADE.

DAY TWENTY-NINE: DRINK IT UP

When Jeff and I first started dating, I thought one of the ways a guy shows you he loves you and is pursuing you is by bringing you your favorite drink from time to time. In all fairness I did grow up in Seattle, home of the coffee bean. (OK, it's totally not the home of the coffee bean, but man do we love our coffee there!). So I frequented coffee shops. And if you know me, you know that one of the ways to my heart is by coffee. Straight up, just bring me a cup of coffee with a heavy dose of creamer and I'll love you forever. Now, Jeff never brought me coffee when we were first dating because of the long distance. The few times we were actually together, he just didn't know that fact about me because, again, long distance. You just don't know those day in and day out things about the other person because you're never around them. If I'm honest with you, I'll say that this did factor into my breaking up with Jeff the first time. I just didn't think he liked me that much. It's a long story, but man, was I wrong. Wrong about Jeff not liking me that much and wrong that true love was summed up in a coffee drink!

I know now true love is about so much more than bringing you your favorite drinks. It's actually more about faithfulness, kindness, forgiveness and grace. However, knowing the little ways that show your person you like them and know them is important too and for me, that's coffee. Jeff knows that about me now and will bring me special drinks from time to time. I still remember the second year of marriage, he came home one day with two Starbucks red cups, the first of the season! Talk about TRUE LOVE!

Today, get your man his favorite drink. Maybe it's coffee like me or maybe it's a soda, Kombucha or a special water. Bring it to him at work, school or have it waiting for him at home. He'll love the kind gesture.

JOURNAL BELOW:

WRITE WHAT YOU LEARNED TODAY, HOW IT
WENT AND WHAT MEMORIES WERE MADE.

DAY THIRTY: GIFTS

I'm not gonna lie. I love getting gifts! Not just any gift but ones that are super thoughtful and so me. When I open a gift from someone and it's exactly what I like, my heart is completely melted because I feel *known* and loved. It doesn't have to be anything big or expensive (I mean, this girl does love her diamonds, but really...). It can be the smallest thing (and honestly sometimes that's even better) like chocolate in a mason jar because those two things are my love language.

One time I had mentioned to my mom how much I love flowers and so I decided every time I go grocery shopping, I'm just going to buy myself a little bouquet of flowers as a treat to myself. Even if it's just one sunflower, it brings me so much joy to see it every time I walk past it or catch a glimpse of it. Since mentioning my love for flowers to my mom, she has brought me flowers every other week. Now, of course, I didn't tell my mom so she would buy me flowers. But because she is the most thoughtful person in the world, she always thinks of me when she runs into Safeway and will buy me a bouquet because she knows how much they mean to me (I know, she's the best)!

As much as I love receiving gifts, I like giving them even more. I love thinking of a gift that would bless someone I love. The best is when I'm out and about and I see something that screams one of my friends or family members. I have to get it. Even if it's a "just because" gift.

Gifts don't have to cost much at all; it can be the simplest thing, as long as it says "I'm thinking of you." Go out today and get a little something for your man. Maybe it's his favorite candy bar, a pair of his favorite socks, a few guitar picks, a new book that he's been wanting or a couple of movie tickets. Anything that says, "You are loved and known."

JOURNAL BELOW:

WRITE WHAT YOU LEARNED TODAY, HOW IT
WENT AND WHAT MEMORIES WERE MADE.

DAY THIRTY-ONE: THANK-FULNESS

It's really easy to complain and think of all the things you'd like to be different right? Unfortunately, this is really easy to do when it comes to your man. There have been times when I let my mind wander and go down rabbit trails of how I'd like Jeff to be different. Or rather, things I'd like for him to do differently. How he can change. Areas he needs to grow in. Things I dislike; areas I get frustrated or irritated by. Yuck! Even just writing this out, I feel trapped and down.

It's good to see areas someone can grow in, to pray for them and encourage them to be the best version of themselves that they can be. It's never good to get in a pit of ungratefulness and complaining. It's toxic and not only will it bring you down, it will bring down the relationship.

Cultivating a heart of thankfulness is so vital in life, as well as in a relationship. Thinking of how thankful you are for your man and listing out ways that you're thankful for him is so important.

Todays task isn't so much for him but for you. Fostering a thankful heart for him will naturally overflow into your relationship and will affect how you see him. This will impact him because you'll become more joy-filled, grateful and kind, instead of complaining, nagging or harboring bitterness. Today list out ways that you are thankful for him. It can be the littlest thing to the biggest thing. Have fun seeing all the ways he is a blessing in your life!

JOURNAL BELOW:

WRITE WHAT YOU LEARNED TODAY, HOW IT
WENT AND WHAT MEMORIES WERE MADE.

DAY THIRTY-TWO: YOUR TURN

You didn't think there was going to be a day 32 did ya? We thought we'd add one more day, to turn it over to you. Think of any idea, any gesture, or any kind thing you can do for your significant other today. Be creative. Be loving. And most of all show them how much you care. Also, we'd love to hear what you picked for day 32! We might even end up including it in future versions or volumes of this book. You can upload your idea at *upload.31creativeways.com*. We can't wait to hear how creative you guys are and what y'all came up with!

JOURNAL BELOW:

WRITE WHAT YOU LEARNED TODAY, HOW IT WENT AND WHAT MEMORIES WERE MADE.

_____

_____

_____

_____

_____

_____

_____

A NOTE FROM US AFTER FINISHING THIS BOOK.

First off, you all rock! For reals. Complete rockstars. Why? Because you care about your relationship. You're investing in it. You believe in it. It matters to you.

We believe that a relationship is like a garden. For it to flourish it needs proper nourishment, constant care, awareness of the things trying to hurt it and sometimes is a little messy. This book is just a start to hopefully continuing or taking that leap of putting you and your significant other on the path to a vibrant and beautiful relationship.

So thank you for doing this journey with us. Thank you for reading this book. And thank you for just being you. We'd love to hear from you and how the challenge went by sharing something online with the hashtag #31creativeways. We are constantly on that hashtag to see all the awesome stuff you guys are doing, ways you tweaked one of our challenges to make it better and to see all the fun you're having!

OTHER RE-SOURCES

For those who maybe are getting this as a gift or don't know much about us, below are just a few other things we have created and done over the past few years. We hope they encourage you!

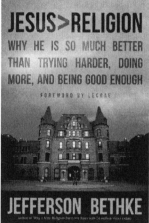

Find at
JEFFBETHKE.COM

Find at
BETHKEWORKSHOPS.COM

WHERE TO FIND US ONLINE.

We love when folks give us a shout on social media,
so feel free to stop by and say hey!
Would love to e-meet you.

 INSTAGRAM

@jeffersonbethke
@alyssajoybethke

 TWITTER

@jeffersonbethke
@alyssajoybethke

 FACEBOOK

fb.com/jeffersonbethkepage
fb.com/alyssajoybethke

 SNAPCHAT

jeffersonbethke

 WEBSITES

jeffbethke.com
alyssajoy.me
bethkeworkshops.com
31creativeways.com

We are always looking for great things to help marriages and relationships. We've found a few we absolutely love and hope you guys will too!

DATEBOX:

We LOVE this. It's a subscription service that sends you a fully curated Datebox every month to your doorstep. For example, during the Christmas season in December we got a box that included a gingerbread making kit, two custom mugs, hot cocoa mix, a Christmas playlist and bunch more goodies. We have a blast every time one shows up on our door. We wanted to hook you guys up to check it out. If you use code 'bethke' at checkout at http://www.getdatebox.com, you get your first month 50% off. Definitely a steal of a deal and something we love!

STRONGERMARRIAGES.COM:

This is a phenomenal website that just has crazy amounts of content to help and build any marriage out there! They have courses, blogs, books and more. It's a site that isn't afraid to talk about real life either, which is so important to us.

Made in the USA
Charleston, SC
04 October 2016